Straddling
the Sibyl

poems by Marc Pietrzykowski

Straddling the Sibyl
Copyright © 2014 by Marc Pietrzykowski

Layout: Marc Pietrzykowski
Front and Back Cover Photos by: Ashley Pietrzykowski

ISBN-13: 978-0615929309
ISBN-10: 0615929303

for more books, visit Pski's Porch:
www.pskisporch.com

Printed in U.S.A

- For Ashley -

Other books by Marc Pietrzykowski

...and the whole time I was quite happy (poetry)
The Logic of Clouds (poetry)
Following Ghosts Upriver (poetry)
Music Box Dancer (fiction)
Conflagrations (poetry, with Mary Leary)
No Tribe, No Tribute (poetry)
The Emissary (fiction)

visit the author virtually at www.marcpski.com

Contents

Section 1

Section 2

Section 3

poems in this collection have appeared in *the Underground Voices, sixfold,* and *Slipstream.*

Section 1

Straddling The Sibyl

O, not on leaves, light leaves, inscribe thy song!
—Virgil

I sit in the ripening shadows of fall
reading what's written on leaves by the wind—
it's the story of me, of course, and that thing
a poet must learn, or else not sing at all:

No whistling, no humming, no rattling of bones

without knowing the fine black edging of rot
that seeps into color—only then can I sing
about failure and beauty, suspicion and sin,
a song made in hope that it's ending might not

spell itself out like a sky full of stones.

Footsteps in the Alley

She smells like rainwater and blueberries:
not enough. She can start a chainsaw,
    draw perfect hands and feet,

drink whiskey like a mathematician,
and still, not enough. The sleepless
    wandering, the lost days,

never enough for the secret world.
The voice beneath the voice, the words
    that buzz the air like winged razors:

the corona of the hidden world, glowing
as the dark spot drifts across the photosphere...
    splashing puddles in her church dress,

her mother's face an orange shriek,
so much like the face of the man
    who choked on corn at the picnic,

so much like the face of every passer by,
every face a comet hurtling into the space
    between galaxies, so cold, they all burn

so cold. Every day she is older, and every day
she keeps us all from drifting away,
    she keeps the secret world secret,

but some days she is so very tired,
and some days she is lost, and some nights
    she wanders, peeks in windows,

makes sure we are safe, or at least
    sleeping.

Cabinet of Wonders

Hefting Mrs. O out of bed required
a winch and a cradle of straps
and a hard ear: she cried, at least
more often than wailing, wordless,
the occasional bark. No wonder,
both hips were shattered, her spine
nearly a question mark.

So, her soft sobs were welcome
Tuesday morning, before bath,
and her sudden shrieks ignored,
at first, until we saw her fist
jabbing toward the floor: a small,
pink, heart-shaped box had fallen
and lay beside the bedpan.

Jamilla opened it, and up sprung
a tiny ballerina, en pointe,
pirouetting to Für Elise,
gears plinking slowly, slowly,
the song Mrs. O's sister practiced
forever, in the front parlor,
the sun colored vase of lilies
atop the piano, hair in a shaggy bun.

We all listened as it slowed
to a crawl, one note, one more,
then hung, unresolved, on the C.

Mrs. O didn't have to cry, Jamilla
turned the key before breathing,
let it play, let it wind down again,
then turned the key once more
to watch the ballerina twirl.

The Mirror Ball

The paranoid stride, the walk of jabbering phone-bent stickmen
on their way to inner glow, to feeling all shiny and right
as they jerk past the ice cream truck,
shimmy past the illuminati outpost,
because all is not right, all is dull, the world
is filled with talktalktalk.

I know where they are going, I have gone there myself.
The shorter of the two once tried to rob me
with a letter opener in the back,
made me feel so bad I gave him a ten-spot and told him,
"it's alright, we all go to t-bone's sometime, tell him I said hey."

I have lived in many rooms, most of them near a dealer
of some drug or other. They're everywhere, as is sensible,
as is right, they offer derangement of the senses,
and the senses offer a curtain of rot spattered with joy.
A fistful of bills gets you a packet of sunlight,

or at least, something to make those spatters shine and wobble
and swell larger than is right. It's not god, it's just dope,
and there's a reason they feed it to child soldiers
before asking them to kill their families, there's truth
in how it makes us dance.

The Panopticon, I: Clockwatcher

*There is one that is alone, and he hath not a second; yea, he hath
neither son nor brother; yet is there no end of all his labor, nei-
ther are his eyes satisfied with riches. For whom then, saith he,
do I labor, and deprive my soul of good? This also is vanity, yea,
it is a sore travail.*
--Ecclesiastes 4:8

Cookies on the table for the meeting, wee napkins
for scribbling the rites of succession, the blood feuds,
the bad haircuts, all the maledictions of the sales clan,
the ones who pull their feet beneath their chairs
to hide their worn and desperate shoes.

The agenda: dream of the day I outlive you all,
put it in the smartphone, mark the date with a ringtone.

The table is smeared and tacky, we try to not rest
our mammoth heads upon it, we fiddle with our hands.
The agenda: look at your caste: abortions, every
last one of them, whoever is droning on about margins
moreso, if only I could have pulled the umbilical cord
tight around your neck, America would smile on,
as the invisible hand pulls us taut, pulls us upright.

Back to my cubicle, O my green foam dreams,
back to staring into the bulb, back to the oracle
and my diorama, O my other world, toward her
I drift, the hot sands for to bury my feet in,
the blare of surf, reeling cabana drunk beneath
the blare now of mountains, of forest untouched.
My hovercar thrums, barely electric, my floating

garden leaks not into the water table, bass and perch
leap into the paddle boat and prostrate themselves.
I am alone and you are alone and it never rains
but rains gently, when it has been hot for too long.
But no, back to the bulb, back to the theoretical world:
Ding! Another meeting. Ding! Another message,
the courier binary insists itself. Ding! The coffee
is warmed, in the breakroom the hyenas surround me,
I am laughing too, there is no end to this laughing
or they will tear me to pieces. We laugh our way back
to the dried-up well, the blurred and sticky table,
the chairs, their fabric clotting, the charts and laser pointer,
the bulb that projects the bulb upon the wall. We stare.

H.R., P.R., V.P., a new brochure to acknowledge. It looks
like a high school yearbook, all those funereal heads.
Best dressed. Most naive. Salesperson of the Quarter.
It is very shiny and makes us want to die.
Or go swimming, in a wicked stream, in a bath of acid,
whatever wipes these faces off our skin, they float down
like ash from the projector screen, they flutter
down from the ticking flourescents and stick to us,
turn to scales, fuse with our skin, every second
we grow more reptilian, more vetted.

The Kings and Queens of our tribe are lizard through and through,
they have completed the transformation and so the stream,
for them, is no place to wash but rather to swim, splash,
pose, dart their tongues, the faces in the brochures
float by and feed them. Their own faces.
Marketing Research. Information Technology. We are mumbling

half-lizard, half-bird abortions, never Kings and Queens,
but still we nest in the necropolis. We work. No one
has the language to do anything else. What we do have:
The bulb. The faces. Unvoiced dreams, green, red,
and otherwise. The alerts, the bells. Casual Fridays. Happy hour.
Secret Santa. Corpses. The end of the motherfucking day.

Internet Porn

Like so much gossip, what the horse cock said
to the sparkling yoni, what the sphincter claimed
the mad dildo had done. Every head
a Rushmore. Every toe a moistened Grand Dame.

Like all gossip, it is a fountain of hate,
no, a lawn-sprinkler, off-center. A room of brown lights.
Scrawl of pimples. Stubble. Cocaine. All hidden, all dissipates,
leaving keyboard and mouse and tissue and the rest of the
screaming night.

I Am the Hairy One

My dental hygienist is a small, middle-aged Russian woman
whose hair is dyed orange and lifted from her scalp
with the aid of spray and brushes. She makes me bleed.

Today, I have a morning appointment. I lay back in the chair
while she snaps on her gloves and bends over me
and I notice her vagina smells terribly strong, and wrong.

I also notice that she's tried to cover the smell with another,
a lilac perfume that lays atop the other smell obliquely,
a bouquet in a jar of vinegar, a garland after corpse-washing.

Normally, I would not draw attention to her suffering,
but I am prone and she is digging at my mouth with a hook
and I cannot turn away; then a third smell, latex, intrudes.

I am told to rinse. I hear my dental hygienist in the hallway,
telling a co-worker she feels faint, she needs to go home and get
the pills she forgot to take. "Once I finish the hairy one," she says.

I am the hairy one. I can't stop saying it. I am the hairy one!
She grinds the polish into my teeth and I rinse again. She is smiling.
Maybe the pills are for her vagina. Maybe I am a bear, dreaming.

Poem For Dolores

The worst part of grieving
is waking up the next morning
and they're still gone, your love,
your friend, your ambitions,
your ideals. And that still, in
the little house beside the stream,
in the penthouse looking down
into the cities' maw,
in the trailer rattled by wind,
still, you have to get up
and make fucking breakfast
    and the breakfast tastes stupid
        because breakfast is stupid,
more of the ubiquity of living,
it all happens here and most
of what happens isn't worth a shit.

But really the worst part of grieving
is waking up weeks later
and forgetting that they're still gone
and you've had breakfast
    and read the paper
        and are on your way to work
before you realize
your grief is slipping away
like everything else, back
into the stream,
into the city crumbling,
into the wind and all the detritus the wind
carries away.

Give 'em Enough Rope

I went in search of devils and demons, not mine,
but fauna, a set of trading cards, Hummelware.
I put them under glass and walked away.

The road took me and I drifted a while,
believing, as drifters do, it was something rare:
to make selves anew, peel them off, and walk away.

Then home drew me back, something I'd left behind
felt immanent, a pole star. The demons were there,
and yes, each looked like me, but I walked on,

into the next room, into a box of toys lined
with black paper speckled with stars, then into the space
between the stars, past Atman, past Brahman.

I waited there for a visitor. None came, or I looked away,
and tumbled out of the box, the room, demon stares
now fixed on me. If only we all had a little more time.

Rational Actors

Isn't it funny: in every city,
in every place and every time
lives someone rich and someone poor
by some clear measure, or so I'm told.

Rise up through the rafters, Lord,
rise up from the floor.

I've seen a few and heard countless more
claim: 'tis the rich what own the stories,
now, if not in aeternum,
and so they must shepherd the rest along,

'tis their duty, 'tis their cross.
By this claim, have and have not
begins to gleam like natural law--
if any two words belong together less

let them speak now, or this: natural law
leaves suicide notes in brown hotel rooms,
on the night stand, in a puddle of gin,
so all the words run together.

Rise up through the rafters, Lord,
rise up from the floor.

But there is no body, detectives
flutter confused, boys from the lab
comb the carpet. Nothing. Only a feeling,
that someone left the room seconds before

the night clerk opened the door;
that someone left the note, some grifter charged
with spiffing up the old lie: wealth justifies itself:
so sayeth the parasites: you know, the rich folks.

Rise up through the rafters, Lord,
rise up from the floor.

The Goad

Morning horror: the montage flickers, but still,
there's no mistaking it, my filth,
shitty second and third takes meant
for the cutting room floor. Metaphor
and self and accretion, coral blooming
then choking in dead water, rooms without
ceilings, with half-walls blasted away.
A new day! Then the task-master speaks,
the collar, the humbler supreme: rise,
you whining piece of shit, rise
and give forth, rise. And most days, we do,
except for certain holidays, improvised,
celebrations of skenographia, orations
from pre-history, wallowing, whatever,
even the filth can entrance, see how cleverly
the montage has assembled itself.

Catullan Calisthenics

The list unspools comically down the castle steps:
the people I would fuck over in exchange
for eternal fame as a poet, acolytes rapturous, wine bottle
stuffed with poppies before my midnight headstone,
twee little cupids with harmonicas, yea, for poesie
my family, friends, mentors, enemies, innocents
and the condemned alike I would gladly offer up
to the invading horde, should posterity anoint me
laureate-outside-of-time. One thing I would not do,
on the very wee, useless, T. Rex-y other hand,
is write the sort of shit that would get me with garland
now, even if I were supple enough to bend thusly,
and my head small enough to get past the sphincter,
the proper pose of a poet, lost in the cave of muses.

Panopticon II: All the World's a Stage and I Can't Stop Saying "MacBeth"

The Certified Personal Success Coach stumbled,
caught his skull on the corner of the podium
and fell, dead as a porterhouse. No, that was the dream,
and somebody shook me awake, my snores
were chewing the rafters. He was still making
word-noises. With a crack, the roof opened and it was night,
stars turning tarentellas, meteors easing through Orion,
but none of it matters because I fail, I cannot
accept responsibility for being a peak performer,
can't take the risks necessary to succeed,
the crowd stares at him with their television faces,
avoiding rapture, avoiding the rub,
and that's why the crowd are winners,
the front of the parade, waving at the slag gathered
in the gutters. Inside the auditorium we are all
the Certified Personal Success Coach but
even better, more beautiful, sexy, assertive, smart, confident,
certain that self-love is a waste of time, the minutes
drip away, there's nothing waiting for us at the end,
past the 401k, past the qualia, all the minutes
droning by in the background like canned music
in a very loud, very stupid hotel bar
full of animatronic italian suits swapping punch words,
bell curves, contempt and conquests, until the music
stops, the lights come up, and the creature of pure appetite
rises to haunt. We assume our positions and exit,
brochures clutched to our breasts,
back to our cubicles, anointed, greased,
thrumming with the numbers we are ready to emit.

Injured Reserve

My face hurts. I'm at the wrong end
of time, the prow, the figurehead, the end
pushing off into the future. Also
because of laughing too hard, too long,
can't even recall what was funny,
and laughter is not medicine at all,
it's a cancer, though it's still "the best."
Either way, my cheeks feel dragged
through gravel and glass, my teeth
are extensions of my spine and I'm
bouncing along in a old carriage,
wheels in ruts, axle oiled with animal fat.
My eyebrows have gone raving. Eyes itch.
But it ain't so bad, really, because
by "face" I mean "species," and by "the future"
I mean all that we've yet to love,
and of course all the carrion, the piles of shoes.

The Wilhelm Scream

Blessed night, blessed wind,
a shovel in gravel squeaks;
I am a slave of demons weird,
of demons burnt chemically clean.

When into an emblematic world
my skull through birth canal squeaked,
there came demons weird and many
to see the mewling meat.

And on that day, the blessed rains
ate away most of the pyre,
and in the wet and stupid soot
the stupid, swaying choir

did mumble on and on and on
the way that all choirs must,
each shape-sung note an aggregate
of aggregated tongues,

of notes inside of notes inside of
thigh bones drilled with holes
to pentatonically ensnare
the demons to their thrones.

And from these chairs, these glory seats,
the demons flick their whips
and think their power infinite--
but we know better, down in the pit.

All The Sad Gods are Sleeping

I began to sign my name to the card and stopped,
left the gifts sitting on squares of colored paper,
the tea kettle whistling, and I walked

into the screaming sun. After a time
it went silent, and the tea kettle still whistling
called me back, the longjing dry and ready.

I bent and poured and felt the steam
trace my face like a blind child.
Some day I will fall away from my throat

with my name in my fist and all the knots
will loosen, and the sun will call me back.
All the gifts will be wrapped and ready, then.

Mobius

The mountain in the rear view mirror
purses its lips and throws me a kiss
and all the cars behind me shimmer
like a breeze-blown curtain
on a late Saturday afternoon, sunlight
stretching its paws up the wallpaper.

And on the mountain, a door, bright red
and brass handled, and behind the door
her skinny toes curling crooked
over the couch arm, a chipped
and dormant teapot, a dusty mirror
reflecting a dirt road that leads away,
a rattling sedan crawling it like a roach.

The face around her mouth (an O
like an eclipse, like a moray's discreet
door, a mineshaft on an asteroid)
is settled as a cairn, and points the way
home. Home was fingertips reading
the story of a spine, and now?
A cardboard motel in a glass desert.

I toss cards at a hat, as I learned to do
from movies full of sharp-faced men
who wait. I toss them to make myself
believe I am waiting, and I am, for a day
unlike any other to come. A day like the one
before the mountain rose, before it was
a dark valley, before molten stone and scattered
bits of star finding each other in the crevices
between past and not-past. The day
it finally goes still, perfectly smooth,
all the jokes told and crevices filled in.

The Panopticon, III: Monster Milk

Yes! I am doing good works, sitting behind an appletini
playing Quick Draw, watching millionaire man-babies
(whose haircut frequency I do covet) sing along
with songs about money, the tune floats out of loudspeakers
hidden in the wall, the sound system comes free
if you subscribe to the feed and the service contract
you pay on time. (Eat nachos). (Watch the large TV and her
many many babies). Don't focus, don't watch, just bathe
in the glow, appletini and LCD, they rhyme, they barely rhyme.
All day I service the landlord, I service the network (I live
to serve), and in the evening, I service the liver, I serve
leers to the shotgirls a-bouncing. I am here for you, agape,
I accept all commercial offers, every sweepstakes, I only
have a few loose hours, when not filling out surveys,
trying to win iPads, servicing, servicing, I am the GDP
and have but one life to give, to live in service of, what luck
this tavern has a multi-out phone charger. This tavern has
one thousand flavors of vodka. I come to serve, even in
the loose hours, even in my "down time." (Down time
is for pussies). I play the jukebox, select from the feed,
more songs about money, the shot glasses twinkle like a city
on a hill. I serve myself shots from the bottle and am,
like so many prophets, misunderstood. (Onward, Patriots!)
God is love. (Onward, through the mirrored walls!) I serve
the bartender, who is pregnant, nigh to bursting with another
man-baby. I can tell it is a man-baby because she is not,
currently and with much aplomb, doing a porno.

And I Am Not Afraid....

I have tasted the flesh of the zombies who live
        behind the gates of work/play communities,
tried to understand them virally, on the scale
        of the scourge. I have supped
with vampire monkeys on rooftop gardens, watching
        helicopters plummet in the sunset
like cherry blossoms.

I have raised my tiny fists in triumph with the over-diagnosed,
        the over-determined half-time celebrants, all
to no avail: my mind's right as rain, Pancho, it's this world,
        this mad, bad, stupid world
that turns my very love for it to maggotry.

Again

I once thought I lived with demons,
that my skin was stretched over a dark, rank hole
littered with whispers and half-burnt photographs.
But I never thought to shoot a child in the face,
then another, moving down the row of their heads
with purpose, a factory arm welding together transmissions.

Instead the dark is what surrounds me and what I heard
was an echo.

I thought I talked to demons and then everything went quiet:
people in mousy coats wandered a muddy field
talking into their phones, staring into the woods and sky,
fingers twitching at the air, looking for little hands,
for asteroids torching the sky, for the horizon to break.

The Hands Struggle Against the Mainspring

The best time to travel, I've heard, is off-season,
when the tourists cannot claim you,
when the gawker arcades are boarded,
the jet-skis all shrink-wrapped and put to bed.

Is that also the best time to stay at home? A bitter
Wednesday in Reykjavik, the Bay of Smoke
a studio backdrop to the trudging of boots
in snow, the chorus begging, "no more fish, please"?

Every time I rise from bed I invade, I plunder,
I am Visigoth because I fight inertia and win,
most days. I plunder the coffee maker. I rape
myself with all manner of picks and prods and wipes.

Even at home I am a tourist, unwilling to learn
the secret language of corners and eaves,
filling the world with iterations of self, each
ugly as the next, each ugly as both those words,

each word yet another iteration, another self.
And so I must escape, out to the sidewalk,
to the airport, searching always for the glorious city
defended by geese, ready to raze it and move on.

After the Political Party

The data are broken, a pile of sticks.
The words, hollowed, carcasses on the forest floor.
Every candle blew out when the door opened.
Gradually our eyes adjusted to the dark.

It smells like a marketplace.
Something crunches underfoot.
From the corner, a keening—we think it might be the corner.
Now, a chorus of wails. Now harmony. Now lies.

Sunlight starts to leak through the doorway.
Eyes meet, embarrassed, we look at our shoes,
at the little bones we've been stepping on.
The tables are full of potsherds, headless dolls,
clipboards, loose cutlery. Ossified breakfasts.

Our numbers dwindle with the day.
The blind sun calls us out.
The inner circle crowds the shadows, behind the podium,
arguing over the evening's seating chart.

The Panopticon, IV: Force of Nature

She rose up in the meeting like a mountain
shearing into being when tectonic plates collided,
she rose and started speaking
and could not stop.

She blazed past the agenda like a comet,
past all the kabuki into the wellspring of resentment,
how everything she hated
was in this room.

She said: *My sun god is not the same as your sun god:*
My Apollo drives a Honda, your Apollo drives a donkey.
My song of science is not the same as your song of science:
Your song is sung by a ghost, my song is sung by a monkey.

All the families that live on all the mountains of garbage
will some day be washed clean by showers of golden light--
if that is the song that lifts you to sleep, well sing away, fools,
and leave my tribe the rest of the night.

The god squad clutched their medallions. The big boss
sucked his teeth. The sales team dreamt of bourbon.
The Hapsburg Empire remained defunct. Aum Shinrikyo
became Aleph. She sat and started a game of solitaire
on her tablet.

She never spoke again, in a meeting or the break room,
and when she died her body turned into a pile of tiny feathers
and drifted out the window
into the street.

Night at the Opera

In my mind like a sty is the boy who spends
his paycheck on tattoos of street gang allegiance
but without first trying to join, or even
moving to the city where the anointed gang lives.

He poses for Facebook, he poses for Twitter,
a fistful of dollars and his grandpa's revolver,
his thorny blonde hair cut close to the scalp,
and nobody knows him, and nobody cares.

Oh how I would love him. His head on my lap
I would stroke and coo 'til he finally slept.
But I know I'll never be allowed to soothe him
as I know he'll never get a call from the crips.

Peripatetic Spiel

The wind shears across the empty park
like scissors through cheap wrapping paper,
scorching my ears and making the dog dance in frantic little steps,
and we go on past a stopped blue van marked "Ryan's Interiors,"
a bald, skinny guy in the driver's seat talking to his phone, or his hand,
but I'm betting on the phone, and then a shovel upright in a snow bank
where someone abandoned their driveway, for now,
and the postal van darts by, on the afternoon package route,
and my right testicle starts to ache, and there is a 98% chance
it's tumorous, and the sky is more bruise than blue
and more black than bruise,
and I stop to breathe it all in and the dog keeps dancing,
and my testicle stops aching and the chance of tumor
recedes back to 0%, and a crow laughs at me from a picnic table,
and I know I'm not supposed to write poems like this anymore
because only 27 people read poetry these days and they
are bored with it but that's OK, I'm not bored with them,
or with the bob tailed squirrel skipping his way across the church roof,
I only wish you were here with me, because it will never
happen this way again, there was only just enough room for everything,
nothing sagged, nothing gaped, nothing askew, the plenum
was apparent and of course it was fucking perfect,
just like every other minute of every day, shooting forth
like a shower of sparks.

The Observatory

The immensity of my head, of the room that surrounds it,
of the house and town and valley and universe and galaxy,
of the space between it all, the way it blooms forth,
is a brood of facts deafening to live among, and oh, the barnyard reek.

And so I don't, or not often, when I do, the shock
is nearly paralytic, and certainly unnatural, I must work,
I must earn my bread. Awe is parasitic, it feeds
by revealing what a pitiable share we're stuck with.

I'm of the infinite, and to know it would surely be grand,
but that's not the same as living, so I defer,
I restrict, I hem, I dawdle as I dwindle, I stand when I should sit,
I look at my skin, glad it's not everywhere all at once.

Future Worlds: Ketosis Mundi

Everyone has a camera in their eye,
        and everyone's camera can see
                everyone else's camera.
That's how the miniature grand dame
        opens her breakfast nook
                to anyone that cares to watch
as she unburdens a fresh scalpel
        of its cardboard sleeve,
                turns it to twinkle in the morning glow,
then slides it gently between
        the second and third segments of her pinky,
                left hand, of course, it takes
almost no effort at all! Thanks to Gorka Knives, LLC.
        Seared in fresh butter, glazed
                with maple and apricot, white pepper,
served atop a bed of locally-sourced leg hair.
        The rest of the cutlery has been in her family
                for all the generations, was buried in a sack
under the floor during 13 different wars,
        and now, with an ancient, gleaming fork pinched
                between the fingers of her right hand,
she holds a glistening slice aloft,
        perfectly bronzed and crunchy on the outside,
                moist and forgiving within;
that small sucking sound we heard
        was 13 million saliva glands kicking on
                as she placed it on her tongue
just below the edge of the camera frame.

Another herd gathers to watch
        news of the latest anaesthetic compounds,
                including a salve tailored exclusively
for the tastebuds of infants:

no more messy extrusion and emulsification
        of mommies' belly and breast and butt fat,
the natural way is always best,
     those tiny fingers and toes were made
        for tiny mouths, dip them in the special applicator
and let them go to town.
     A smaller gaggle, in one of the eye's many corners,
        gathers to complain about long hours
spent in the immersion tank
     regrowing bits of tendon, genitalia, lobes and lids;
        though some customers want the tasty bits,
most dine out to feel served, waited on,
     but really, some people, so rude,
        and you go and slice away your calf
and one or both ears, and the stupid, drunk cook
     burns it, I mean, they know we work for tips,
        god forbid a church bus pulls in,
little old ladies clutching their ourobros pendants,
     cutting their eyes at unnecessary children--
        they tip worse than shit farmers.

Just prior to evening ablutions, the washing of the eye,
     one of the candidates for Lead Geneticist
        commandeers a chunk of vision
to offer platitudes. I don't know why
     they can't just leave us alone,
        stop intruding, we have chosen already
to be free, and freedom-loving,
     we have no need of a Moloch,
        of a great maw to mash us to pap,
no need for a wheel of samsara to grind us to dust:
     we have swallowed Moloch whole,
        and the only wheel that matters
is the one our heroes turn,
     the great contortionists, those captains of industry
        with spines preternaturally supple--

even as children, it is said, they could bend
        to get their lips and teeth around
                their own greatest delicacies,
the choicest sliver of colon, the steaming fresh shit.
        They are icons of grace, ever rolling,
                ever turning, ever eating, of themselves, amen.

Claudette Colbert as Cleopatra (1931)

"The queen is testing poison."
Calm words in quiet halls--
run, man, run!

A scroll from the foot of a pigeon:
War. An inopportune moment
For the pigeon-keeper.

On the day of the moon? Some deeds
move better on a day whose night
has no moon.

Trumpeters blow and warships
break anchor and night
is lit and churning with bodies.

The asp moves the tulips.
The servant girl steps quick,
scoops it into a jar.

Slowly the wind
stills. Death and night and blood
in black and white.

The Long Night of Fubar Bundy

Having spent the day worrying about trees, and cancer,
and his job, and the future of the species, and his job,

Bundy squatted in a pile of bones and tilted his head
to watch a cloud of grackles rippling neuronally

across the sky. Even when the light is off, the light
is on, somewhere, and the light glared up from

the chalk-white sprawl of rib, talus, mandible, ulna;
he rubbed his thumb in a femur's fovea, spread his hand

around the head, hefted it like a cutlass, and thrust it
into the sun. The sun began to hiss and sag, the grackles

screamed and swarmed the bone's hilt, an orange jelly
seeped down into the sky and along the tops

of the mountain. Bundy took to his heels, back out
of the valley and through the door of the first cabin he saw,

dark teeth nipping at his ankles. He leaned against the door
and stared back at the wooden faces of men and women

who kept on chewing, said nothing, dipped their spoons
again and still said nothing. The jig is up! Bundy

heard a grackle scream, these are hard people, scabbed
and worn and sun-lovers all! He heard and smiled, his smile

grew, went back to his ears and beyond till the corners
touched each another at the back of his head and froze.

One of the men stood, still chewing, and knocked the top
of Bundy's head off with a spoon. It fell to the floor

and burst into a thousand mice that swarmed back up
along his body and down his throat, a shrouded hole,

a mineshaft. Deprived of eyes, ears, tongue flapping
fishily on his jaw, Bundy supposed he was still there,

standing against the door, not being cut up and put
in a pot with carrots and onions, but his brain too

was a rodent horde working it's way through his small
intestine, so hereness was a problem, but it could not be,

there was something there to worry at it, his body
might be thinking, his body might be mostly steam

and something else was thinking him, had been forever,
had worried about cancer and why the boss squinted

over the tops of his glasses and oh of course the bomb
and the pandemic and the oceans of garbage, body

or not, Bundy was worrying and winding his guts
in a knot, guts or not. The first sound that said

your ears are here was the sound of gnawing,
and the next was a slurp, and then Bundy felt a tongue

poke the corner of his eye. Your eyes have come home,
he pushed the dog away, it came back to lick again,

he let it clean his face. The night was turning to pearl
at the edges. The sidewalk was wet. Bundy sat up.

A long green car drifted along the street. A squirrel
stopped to stare at him, chewing, staring, chewing,

put its head between its legs, turned into a pine cone,
and rolled off. Bundy checked his watch, saw

it was early Saturday morning, nearly time for cartoons,
and that his head was back, intact, but filled now

with the same species of hangover that makes God
murder newborns. The sun peeked at him,

saw no bones, no femur, and blared like an air horn.
Well played, Bundy thought. Revenge makes the grass grow.

Three of a Kind

The banker straddles a hobby horse,
chomps a binky like a maduro,
shits himself and feels the sting,
the whip, the gleaming boot heel, next.

A broken garden gnome, conical hat
half crushed, skull full of spider babies,
presides over a snarl of clover
and the bones of two rhododendrons.

The broom straw scrapes the marble,
thousand-year grooves, scratches echo
up to the saints. She crosses herself, goes home,
changes the paper in the toucan's cage.

Section 2

How Will We Serve the Homunculus?

The Homunculus, Sir, in however low and ludicrous a light he may appear, in this age of levity, to the eye of folly or prejudice;--to the eye of reason in scientific research, he stands confessed--a Being guarded and circumscribed with rights.--The minutest philosophers, who by the bye, have the most enlarged understandings, (their souls being inversely as their enquiries) shew us incontestably, that the Homunculus is created by the same hand,--engendered in the same course of nature,--endow'd with the same loco-motive powers and faculties with us:--That he consists as we do, of skin, hair, fat, flesh, veins, arteries, ligaments, nerves, cartilages, bones, marrow, brains, glands, genitals, humours, and articulations;--is a Being of as much activity,--and in all senses of the word, as much and as truly our fellow-creature as my Lord Chancellor of England.--He may be benefitted,--he may be injured,--he may obtain redress; in a word, he has all the claims and rights of humanity, which Tully, Puffendorf, or the best ethick writers allow to arise out of that state and relation

– Laurence Stern

We seem to imagine that there is some place inside "my" mind or brain where "I" am. This place has something like a mental screen or stage on which images are presented for viewing by my mind's eye. In this special place everything that we are conscious of at a given moment comes together and consciousness happens. The ideas and feelings that are in this place are in consciousness, and all the rest are unconscious. The show in the Cartesian theater is the stream of consciousness, and the audience is me.

– Daniel Dennet

The mind is built from ideas that are, in one way or another, brain representations of the body.

– Antonio Damasio

Proem

We might begin with a man remembering
when he was a child, among the maundering gods
and goddesses so tall he barely knew their faces,
and we might testify how quickly they shrank,
how quickly they grew stupid, how soon
he too grew, dwindled, dried up, fell to earth, the places
his body steered through, the scuffs and marks he left
fading; someone tries to recall his name, draws a blank,
and the blank grows into a new moon...

or, we might focus on the man's body as driven
by the miniscule man who lives in his head,
homunculus, child of Zosimos,
the mech pilot, the one wagging the man's arms
with his own tiny arms, peeping out
through double screens--the backs of a pair of hazel eyes--
his throne tinted hazel, his face a green pout,
his own eyes murderous, gleaming red,
though he's too tiny to do any real harm.

We could, but memory is a filthy lens,
so the homunculus himself (always full of schemes)
suggests, instead, we take a man piece by bloody piece:
head, arms and hands, torso (upper and lower),
legs and feet, each section that extends
outward from self, from the half-remembered dream
that accretes and falls away, but is power
incarnate nonetheless. Each portion is a chapter,
and each part of the homunculus bespeaks the whole.

To this theme, self and pilot, together, up on bricks,
add theme two: the new world, there is always a new world,
but in this case, the first decades
of the twenty-first century, jesus standard time:

yea, we speak across oceans, are even hurled
across them, yea we are a digital mob,
verily we lynch and champion by clicks;
where the two meet, homunculus and technology,
shall be the subject of this essay which sometimes rhymes.

The Head

Born into light, eyes blind to the stuff of the world,
we learn to see, to see from deep in the skull
as though from the bottom of a well,
or pressed up against our eyes, pushing,
unable to break through and shatter the spell
that traps us on the other side. Color and form,
movement, that which is empty, that which is full,
the dorsal and ventral streams gushing,
the occipital lobes each learning themselves awake.

Every nerve winds its way back, every nerve speaks
the language of synapse, the same lexicon
borne by every cell and every cell a child
of the first. Genes flip off, genes flip on,
and lo! Color and form, movement, eyes that seek
props for the theater, ears weaving a score,
tuning in the pit. 'Tis a nervous system indeed
turns oxygen, carbon, hydrogen, and nitrogen
into Chauvet cave, Apollo, Babi Yar.

And the brain is the heart of it, Anaxagoras
might say, the lake upon which we glimpse the nous
staring back, homunculus sees the homunculus
because we are not a dog or tree.
The little man inside surely loves a parade
and so, dances, as minds from other ages float by:
shamanic vessels burping with earth and sky,

sleep and dream, a fetid, roiling brew
drunk from skull cups in a deathless shade;

then the psyche, trebly formed: thymos,
menos, the aforementioned nous, each one orbiting
the other, spinning their way down to Hades,
riding the soul's last breath like a note in a bottle
on an tidal wave, while Plato and Aristotle
jostle for position, poking, I will turn this car
around if you don't behave. The nephesh, blown
by ruach, flaps from the antenna. Galen plays charades
but no one guesses "ventricle." Al-Kindï enthrones

abstraction, Alfäräbï lays ta'aqqul at her feet,
and Averroes turns her spectral, passive,
immaterial, vertices of self cloud the street
like confetti. Who let Chuang-tzu in?
Enough with the jokes, yes, the Tao is massive,
that is, microscopic. He's only come to meet up
with some Dogon split souls, they'll head for the park
and try to fill the reservoir with psilocybin.
Just as well, they can keep Augustine busy.

Soon the spare crowd swells into a throng,
faces flowing by like sunlight on water:
is that Dante? Wearing a tall, narrow house
as a gown? And Ficino, in his Plato t-shirt,
the whole of the renaissance flooding behind,
Petrach, Cusanus, Bruno—a river of faces,
we peep one—Shakespeare! Descartes!--but not for long,
a smell of rust and blood in the air, and the mob
is restless, hungry, they hunt perverts

and find only brothers and sisters
in every alley. Their homunculi dream of work,
and wake dissolute. A flatbed of corpses,

then another; ideas float free: machine soul,
factory soul, computer soul, soul as clerk
of the genetic ledger...and the crowd surrounds,
the parade congeals, consumes, homunculi
shudder and dissemble into singularity.
We must climb free from each new heaven, as from a hole.

But no matter, heaven is a miser's affliction.
What vector to follow otherwise, what tack?
KantLockeHumeFreudJungSarteSearle?
Disaggregate buddha path? Bell's inequality?
It is good to rub and polish our brain against that
of others, the wee man inside twirls
faster, faster, forward in all directions!.
But the homunculus is no centrifuge,
the danger: will he simply fly to pieces?

Or could the distribution of self,
the messages hopping across sea and sky,
the theater of mind entangled
with lines of code, or something better than line,
better than synapse, then grafted back onto the eye
until all eyes are one eye, each self a cell,
save the little man from such dissolution?
The man himself says they're just stories we tell,
more parlor tricks, more stays against confusion.

Arms and Hands

I follow my shadow, near day's end,
arms articulate down from the trunk, hands from the arms,
fingers from the hands, in slanting light distended.
I lift them up and see past them to the trees,
their limbs and branches articulate,
unbraiding the sky beyond them for as far

as they can reach. With arms and hands much like these
we've flung ourselves past that sky, past what trees dream,
so the homunculus might live in a vale of stars.

The thumb is a fulcrum, it gives sense
to the fingers, and the fingers give purpose
to the thumb. A little family, coiled into a fist
or waving from atop the Queen's arm, shaking
and stroking and patting and poking and breaking
and holding another, scratching the surface
of a clay tablet, guiding a laser through
a tumorous lobe: hands extend from the mind
as self from soul, so we claim we've built what we've accrued,

and explain away destruction as irrational,
evil a banality, or less, of animals--
but destruction is as much a symptom of order
as any cathedral. Those slabs of marble
we wear into reverent grooves must first be torn
from the sides of mountains; even the mortar
which holds the raised arch aloft is born
of the prisoner's dilemma: what I want
and the other fucker wants, snarled together.

And thus we persevere, painting mimbre bowls,
machining carburetors, learning to shake hands like
Thraseas and Euandria, all 27 bones
plus whatever sesamoids your folks gave you
wriggling in unison, hefting a stone
like Cain, Theseus, or Shazada Saleem,
calming the face of a child mid-scream,
inserting cannulae that potassium chloride
might speed forth into the waves another soul.

I have an xray of a hand, taken by a hand
with a wondrous machine built by many hands,

and I look, and am afraid of my vision,
that the things of the eyes might intrude
so far into the homunculus that the hands
might wither and fall away; of what use are hands
when we have electroencephalograms
to help us steer our chairs, to change the channel,
to find love, to reach the stars, to gather food?

Then I remember the homunculus acts
within evolution the way water eats at rock:
our eyes see the pocked surface, the cleaves,
not the centuries of waves and mist.
I am no seer, no matter what my own little man believes,
my own frightened little man, stirring up dark water
with a finger, pretending the muddy swirls can talk.
It's tricky, handing the future over to a ghost,
holy, friendly, egui: never the one we'd wished.

It's not entirely the fault of the hands and arms,
this perceptual trick, whereby our experience
predicts and compels and warps the world
into the fun house mirror on which we depend,
but nor are they blameless. The homunculus
must touch to contain, must hold to know what might be lost,
there are no burdens without lifting,
nothing comes to the mind separate from its host;
we are caught by hands when into life we are hurled.

Thus, the fear that we might evolve into bug-eyed heads
with limbs dangling and atrophied from the chin
emerges from a mind created by the body,
by hands and arms, by fingers that make
shadow puppets on the wall, elbows that bend
to send knuckleballs fluttering. We might jettison
the body, but likely all at once, instead
of letting it whither; one mad leap from meat and bone

to nutrient soup seems a likelier end.
Perhaps selves afloat and bodiless
will dream of hands, of having a means to point,
but only as long as self persists, unmoored.
Let me tell you, then, future human living detached
from the homunculus: there is grime under my nails
from changing a bike tire, and my knuckle joints
ache a bit from arthritis, and I know the tips still
smell faintly of onion because I just scratched
my nose. I hope you aren't too bored.

Torso, Upper and Lower

The trunk contains the offal, or, most of it,
the squishy bits, from thorax down to rectum,
lovely seared with a nice chianti. In sum,
the torso is the engine that lets the arms
build cathedrals around any space
the head decides might best house its own issue.
The head would rather not acknowledge its debt,
and the hands and arms are always so busy,
so the torso thrums on, largely unnoticed.

Until it breaks down, of course, and then
whoa, it's the main character, an unreliable
narrator confused by arteries full of plaque,
lungs coated with coal dust, liver turning stool black,
the pyramid scheme called "life" finally collapsing.
Which of us takes time each day to listen to their heart?
Those with heart problems. It's not too late to start,
but the head has all that smart apparatus
for reading the world, the arms and legs all the glamour--

well, not all. The womb glows like nothing else can;
gestation is a period of unparalleled
comfort in most peoples' lives. The parts of the torso

that most loudly demand attention? Those that produce
more of us. Every homunculus began
as a blueprint in a tiny slug of meat,
and the factory ran all night, for nine months,
until the host was extruded and started to bleat.
Yucky? Sure, what happens afterward? Even moreso.

Also miraculous, as with the lower torso
and all its mythological emissions.
Moist parts joined, function meeting form, not much
to see, only the quiver that turns to light
and swells louder than the sun, thicker than night.
The homunculus cannot staunch the swelling,
snared by a glance, a casual touch
that starts the engine racing: the whole torso
at full volume, overclocked, on fire.

And here the head wants to build a history,
a taxonomy, some formula explaining why
we do this: fifty gigabytes of porn per second,
worldwide. The shepherd swains do dance and sing
and every other possible thing,
yet the homunculus is no more fecund,
encircled everywhere by people fucking,
not prudish, simply bored. Not a bang,
but an old libertine sigh, ah god, I've done it all.

A good thing that the orgasm is so cosmically
silly. Don't believe it? Try masturbating
while looking in a mirror: we've not evolved
past that face, the rolled back eyes (if you're doing it right),
the waste of shame, the dreams of fair Troy
or Verona or, sure, Atlantis. Tender is the night
when the queen moon bends down to kiss her fair boy,
and no less comical for it's tenderness; we all
can be queens, able to bequeath love, pleasure, and joy

but ah, life, the homunculus says, gets in the way.
So, back to the factory, back to the grind,
though even the grind is good, if we listen:
The heart beats. The nerves whine. The lungs wheeze away.
And all of it hanging from the spine
in the most beautiful sack of skin
history ever bore witness to: your skin,
your spine, your lungs, your heart beating up through time
like no beat before or after. Yours.

And no, I'm not just trying to get in your pants,
that's the homunculus speaking, paranoid
little wastrel, jealous of his own constituent
parts, except when in thrall to them: always.
He says: I'd sing the stomach, but it's the tongue that wants;
I'd sing the liver, but the brain needs a drunk.
I'd sing of sperm and ovum, testes and womb,
but without the head, the torso's but a tomb.
Of course, the mind is pudding, minus the trunk.

And as the mind persists in its dream
of living without body, a string of code
or some more clever form to render formless
arms, hands, torso, legs, feet, all of it,
the trunk, too, has its dream: machined parts,
extruded, grown on a lattice, a body unbowed
by time, until every organ is rebuilt
endlessly, the cyborg, homo facturus.
Soon enough, it would build a brain: infinite regress.

Legs and Feet

The homunculus cannot escape,
but it can set the body roving
on legs that lift the head above the grass line,

point it toward a horizon that's always moving
away. From a peak in Darién
the ocean looms, and past the ocean,
more peaks, more ocean, ice, sand, and always, more of us.
We are everywhere, a stumbling chorus,
because everywhere we are born and die in motion.

The noise of wooden wheels clattering through ruts in clay,
the axles oiled with tallow, find echo in
the rattling engine, of cars mounted with cameras
to map the world, frame after frame. If the wheel
is an extension of the foot, then the road
is an extension of our need to explore,
to know what the horizon conceals
and learn who holds the whip: we cannot ignore
what goads us, we are ridden and must obey.

Bipedal on the veldt, for provisioning
or warning display or heat regulation
or all of these: bipedal in the city,
waiting for the light to change, pumping pedals
on a bicycle: bipedal at the train station,
boarding the three-nineteen to somewhere shitty:
bipedal in the car, in the plane, in the rocket ship...
arthropodic legs might have made us better jumpers,
but thigh knee crus ankle foot give us vision.

We walk, and think, and search for clues in the eyes
of others walking and thinking, then revise
the homunculus accordingly.
Theory of mind works both ways, recursively,
our selves in others reflected back,
a widening gyre of selves and songs of self:
the story of our journey through time.
There would be no telling if we could not move,
no horizon summoning us, no language, no love.

From identification to temporality
to causality to goals, we learn and walk and learn:
there's a frog here... Here's a moon. These are boots.
We build the homunculus from its constituent parts,
the metonymy of personality,
and my little man and your little man are in cahoots.
We've already reached the singularity,
we're born into it, it stares back at us from the hive,
says: you'll never get out of my gaze alive.

So to fever dreams of evolving beyond, I say,
not without a body that recognizes itself
as body, not without mind falling away
from the work of orientation into
the galaxy of signs: step by step
her feet, the sidewalk, across the quad,
up the stairs, pondering the data, the broad
variations in autosomal loci,
the Toba catastrophe theory,

wondering if mitochondrial Eve, too,
wandered the Paleolithic veldt
lost in her thoughts, snapping back in time only
when the brush rattled or a bird screamed.
Or maybe she turned to face another human who
touched her arm, and smiled, and pointed East,
the route of dispersal, toward the rising sun,
toward the other world and the ocean of dreams
and plenty that lay beyond, always beyond.

And the homunculus stares through her eyes like a cat
sitting in a window watching cars go by,
peering across the synaptic cleft,
and the cars are neurotransmitters
discharging people at receptors
like the mall, the school, the church, the home,

long-term potentiation, yes, thou art that,
and that is in motion, now and forever,
on earth or beneath it, in water or sky.

The homunculus begs for one last turn,
swears we sleepwalk on the cusp of something new:
what of quantum teleportation?
Or the biological-digital converter?
Surely they will release the little man from his cage!
Sorry, there is but one release, no matter which path
we travel, withering away or spurning
the body for ascension of pure mind up a flue
of stars: in transcendence, obliteration.

Section 3

Jelly Oath

I've lived a terribly beautiful life.
I've done everything perfectly. To wit:
I saw a man bent with palsy, his face
gleaming with drool, and I covered my head
and ran past him, hid behind a ficus,
and watched him sob. I was 4, maybe 5,
could tie my shoes, but still was terrified
of public bathrooms. It was exactly
right, and the next time it happens, it will
happen just the same. Years later, I spit
on a grey pigeon in a fit of pique,
and a woman walking by spit on me.
Perfect. Correct. Every sparrow falling.
Still later, I took my war on terror
commemorative pocket comb out
and showed my niece how to extract pepper
from salt. Some day, her kids might live in space,
or as a maze of code on a server,
and I might be here to watch them sail off,
or not, either way: I have lived the most
achingly beautiful life. The best one,
in my admittedly limited view.
I wasn't here, then I was. What the fuck!
I've still not gotten over it, this place,
this name, these eyes, these ears, my god, these feet!
There's nothing intelligent or designed
about me, I'm a goddamned miracle.
And someday, I will never have happened,
a thing even more beautiful, all told.
Sometimes I wish I could see the postscript,
but I'm just being foolish, as is right,
and perfect, and is the best way to live.
I'm no longer afraid of public bathrooms,

and I've spit on other pigeons, and, well,
truth be told, I have never owned a comb.
But I am full, and everything is full,
and has happened, and will happen again
until it stops, so never mind, listen:
the song, how it gathers and does not rise
to any crescendo, how no codas
are possible, not even this: I lived.

Vagrancy is a Characteristic of the Species

Spring thaw arrives, the real one, no more feints,
and Ed is on his porch across the street
smoking and coughing and scowling at trees.
It's a scowl he's been growing all his life,
I've seen photos of it as a seedling,
beneath a crew cut, atop worn short pants.
He scowls at fat robins, at cars, at me;
I smile back, knowing he is kind, and so,
frightened. The next day is rain, the next hail,
then a morning of sun putting its hand
beneath our chins, lifting our heads to see.
Ed is not scowling; I notice his porch
sags at one corner, that shingles are torn.
The school bus pauses, children disembark
and scatter, but still no Ed, no smoke cloud.
I wish I could say I did not forget,
that I went and attended my neighbor,
and sped him to the emergency room,
or found his body face down on the floor,
but it was only months later I heard
of the weeks he spent plugged into the wall,
that he died in a the middle of the night,
so the last thing he heard was some machine
bleeping away, announcing another
change in the ledger. His sister told me
the story, leaning on the porch railing,
the first blind idiot day of summer
bearing down. She had a rag on her head
and a mop in her hand, and her smile said
she would die smiling, if only because
she knew there was nothing to smile about.

Career Interest Survey

I think I'd have made a good pro wrestler,
a heel, of course, a remorseless, taunting
bastard, but diabolical, sneaky,
no foaming at the mouth or purple tongues.
I might ride a bright purple Cadillac,
white seats, with some kind of pink-haired chauffer
up front, top down, yes, a convertible.
I might sing, a torch song, sequins pouring
from my arms and hips like a waterfall,
muscled talons for hands, Lady Macbeth
screeching her approval from the front row.
And then I would lay down on that white seat
and give birth to a tiny, winged imp
that would lick itself clean of placenta
and fly up above the crowd, circling,
waiting for my signal: come child, come perch.
Later, when all seemed lost, when the milquetoast
nearly had me pinned, the imp would swoop down
and peck the smarmy bastard's eyes from his head.
After the match, I'd head up to the roof
and set him free, though he'd not want to leave,
wee tears falling, burning holes in the pitch.
I'd have made a mediocre vice cop
and a terrible oceanographer,
dreamt once I managed the Chicago Cubs,
but if there was no poetry to write,
I would likely stay in bed forever,
or at least until some psychiatric nurse
came to roll me over, pick the maggots
out of my bedsores, and drug me stupid.
I'd have been a terrible marine,
a fair farmer, a good trash collector,
but nothing counterfactual lives here:

the light in the window changes, each day
a struggle to remember: from which field
did I sprout, which galaxies were my eyes,
what eyes preceded the idea of sight:
all that I've never been, trees racing by
in the train window, the itch I can't reach.

Dancing With the Shit People

I danced with them for as long as I could,
in one of their shit houses, not sure whose,
in some shit suburb, some shit cul-de-sac,
where someone slid the coffee table away
and we danced amidst the reek of disinfectant.
They scoured every room eight times a day
'til their hands shrunk, wrinkled, fading to grey,
but no matter, the whole place stunk of shit.
Dinner was superb, all locally sourced
and deftly presented; one of our hosts
was a graduate of the C.I.A.
That it smelled and tasted vaguely of shit
wasn't a big deal, once you stopped gagging,
and once another host taught us a trick:
if you squeeze your left thumb, you can suppress
the gag reflex. An old porn star technique,
though of course I was never a porn star
myself, ha ha, and we all laughed and burped.
Then we had a digestif, then we danced!
Madly, to some shit music that was dull
and over-familiar, but we felt bad
so we flung ourselves about and hollered
and made a racket and acted stupid.
We thought it would please them, would prove
how much we'd enjoyed their shit company,
but they just stared, and shuffled their shit feet,
and then a few of them started to cry.
It's very hard to watch shit people cry.
You can comfort them, make them feel better
for a few hours, but nothing you can say
will ever convince them what's obvious:
they're only made of shit because they're scared
of being anything else, it's all they've known

because they don't want to know anything else,
that their shit parents and shit grandparents
were well meaning fools, that all their totems
and prayers and kisses and yes, all these tears
only cake the shit on thicker, until
no one remembers where it all came from,
and everyone believes they're nothing but
shit, shit, shit, inside and out, all the way through

Close Cover Before Striking

The gods of electromagnetism
came blasting through town last night, furious
and crackling, filling the night with the sound
a tree hears when an axe splits it. A gift,
a ward to dispel all those absurd stories
our parents told us to hide their cowering:
gods bowling, moving furniture, dancing,
or clouds bumping into one another.
A gift: more terrifying than idiot gods:
we've done it to ourselves. Yes, dear Pogo,
the enemy is us, whether we seek
to rule, to own, to squander, to protect,
to preserve, to rescue, obliterate,
hide, sneer, frighten, love, bear, taste, forget--
not one among us can cast the first stone.
We've shit in our cage so long, and so well,
we've taken to eating it, cramming it
in our ears, making it into jewelry,
but now, a gift: blast the scales from our eyes,
turn them to ash in a gush of lightning,
tear them off with tornadoes and hurricanes,
let a few more of us see what we've done
and give them reason to fight, and to live
beside the soured river, beneath skies
twisting with vapor, telling a new tale
to their children: once we cared for nothing,
and nothing cared very deeply for us,
and then we learned to do less harm, but still
babies will be born who seek only to rule.
Those are the ones whose skulls we dash on rocks.

Resting on a Bald Spot

A wolf will walk a thousand miles to eat people; a dog half way to
heaven will still eat dung.

--chinese proverb

A man alone versus the universe
Hooray, man conquers all! Or call bullshit,
the superhero spiel just makes us weak,
we who live and die in the troposphere.
Whether in capes and tights, crown and scepter,
astride a bear, back from some nameless war,
we would do better to ignore them all
and worship ourselves, or even better,
the neighbors we loathe, each legendary
as a madwoman dancing on glass shards,
as a miser unable to escape
the black dog come to drag him from his bed.
What need have we for glory, for grandeur?
Does some clerk scribe the names of those who die
bravely, chastely, as unaware of our
admiration as they are heedless of it,
supermen, walking stoically through rain,
through a rain of arrows, mocking fool death?
Then surely the clerk's partner across the desk
has the more difficult task, scratching down
the names of all the rest of us, the meek,
the shameful, the unforgiving, the crass.
Our craving for heroes is circular,
they hold what is fine just out of our reach
to make us want it more, though not enough,
so the circle becomes Shem for a Golem
formed from the clay we shed when failing to love
the jealous ravings, the night sweats, even
that piercing glint of hatred. A meadow

strewn with lovingkindness is the reward
of those who can but lay beneath the clouds,
expect nothing, and find it everywhere.
The rest must imagine something better.

First Please Register With the Board

Who's in charge here? Who's piloting this ship?
Attention! I'd like to make a complaint.
I hope you notice that I didn't say "please."
But, I did say "you." Oh goddamnit all.
There are only three ways I know how to pray.
Lying's one, since truly there are many.
Countless skulls full, ready to rally the troops.
First the word, then we set your hearts on fire.
Hearts and blood, hearts and blood, back into the mud.
There's a lesson: that God is each other.
Hearts and blood, hearts and blood, flowers in the mud.
That's how we finally feed the monster.
It makes no sense, but it does allow for grace:
more than in a cold glass of lemonade,
more than kestrals hovering in a draft,
more than every mother loving at once
every child that woke in the dark, alone,
and so much more than blood or breath or bone.
It's all included, yet I rage to name it.
Every name makes me think I've been cheated.
Every name flopping like trout on the dock.
Even a suggestion box would comfort
those of us so afflicted we can't speak
without thinking about what we're saying,
and who we're saying it to, and how loud,
and how odd that we came to speak at all,
that we came alive in an ocean of grace
unable to sense any more of it
than the crash of waves on distant rocks.

Skin Like a Rudder, Heart Like a Sail

I imagine it's true, the dogs have gone to the dogs
and the mount straddles the rider, and I care
and I don't, by turns, but one beacon glows
amidst the churning: your eyes, open to the waltzing
stars, drawing me to you like a slip making a beeline
for shore, where a party waits. Too many fools
already cloud the gazebo, someone has found bongos,
and the wine is made from rhubarb and chum
but it's a party nonetheless, and already you've fled
to the woods. The sound of the party dies
behind a curtain of green, I follow, hunt the bent
branches, flattened bracken, startled ferns,
the wet noses of lost congressmen, a jury
is flushed from beneath a log, I stop to rest
on a stump and it tries to sing and make me read
its screenplay. I hear you laughing. It's not funny,
but it is because, only because, you are laughing,
so I fumble on into a creek bed full of gurus,
indignant when I step on their toes, indignant
when I do not, and then war emerges from behind
a pile of stones and a squadron of drones
wraps it in plastic. I stop to view the dead, pressed
like steaks in styrofoam trays. I know the faces,
I know their eyes, every angle and shade and timbre
thrums a dirge, the stump joins in behind me,
from everywhere that music that will drown us all,
the one played as the credits roll, the one
that rattles to an end. I've lost you. No. I can feel
you watching me, from atop an elm, from beneath
the marsh full of fund managers comparing scars,
from within the stink of plastic jaws about to snap shut,
from behind all the jellyfish that have suddenly
blotted out the sun—there you are, your eyes

pulling me into a clearing, laying me down,
laying beside me, fitting my body like a jewel
in its case. I have nothing for you, I was worried,
no matter: *rest, then rise, there is another party up ahead.*

Fugitive

Grey sky, nearly white, the grey road
covered with grey cars rippling past
the grey meltwater swelling the creek,
and the only color is in billboards: fix
your transmission, buy a cheeseburger,
divorce yourself, dingy orange letters
struggling greyly in the afternoon, too early
for turning on the neon. There's no helping it,
no savior, just snow and rain taking turns
trying to freeze or drown us, fragile creatures
all, dimly dreaming, facing forward, in cars
hurtling grey, marking time with the wipers.
But we need no help, amidst so much beauty
it blinds us, turns us lame, leprous,
distracted, because we could not survive
otherwise, all would break into blossom
and none would stoke the fire, all
would die smiling, and truly no one,
no matter what they say, likes that story.
We're allowed just enough to keep the foot
on the pedal, a glimmering at the edge
of grey skies, a burst of light from within
that says: behold, grace in every part,
and in every part, thou, beholding.

Marc Pietrzykowski lives and works in Niagara County, NY.
This is his sixth book of poems.
You can visit Marc virtually at **www.marcpski.com**

Pski's Porch Publishing was formed July 2012, to make
books for people who like people who like books. We hope
we to have some small successes.
www.pskisporch.com.

Pski's Porch

323 East Avenue
Lockport, NY 14094
www.pskisporch.com

www.ingramcontent.com/pod-product-compliance
Lightning Source LLC
Chambersburg PA
CBHW060416050426
42449CB00009B/1988